Why
do people fight
Wars?

Ali Brownlie & Chris Mason

HODDER
Wayland

an imprint of Hodder Children's Books

© 2001 White-Thomson Publishing Ltd

Produced for Hodder Wayland by
White-Thomson Publishing Ltd
2/3 St Andrew's Place
Lewes
BN7 1UP

Other titles in this series:
Why are people racist?
Why are people vegetarian?
Why do people drink alcohol?
Why do people gamble?
Why do people harm animals?
Why do people join gangs?
Why do people live on the streets?
Why do people smoke?
Why do people take drugs?

Series concept: Alex Woolf
Editor: Philip de Ste. Croix
Cover design: Hodder Children's Books
Inside design: Stonecastle Graphics Ltd
Consultant: Jenny Bailey of the Brighton Peace
        and Environment Centre
Picture research: Shelley Noronha – Glass Onion
        Pictures
Indexer: Amanda O'Neill

Published in Great Britain in 2001 by Hodder
Wayland, an imprint of Hodder Children's Books

The right of Ali Brownlie and Chris Mason to be
identified as the authors have been asserted by
them in accordance with the Copyright, Designs
and Patents Act 1988.

British Library Cataloguing in Publication Data
Brownlie, Ali and Mason, Chris
  Why do people fight wars?
  1.War 2.War - Moral and ethical aspects
  I.Title
  172.4'2

ISBN 0 7502 3714 7

Printed and bound in Italy by
G. Canale & C.S.p.A. Turin

Hodder Children's Books
A division of Hodder Headline Limited
338 Euston Road, London NW1 3BH

Picture acknowledgements

The publisher would like to thank the following
for their kind permission to use their pictures:
AKG Photo, London 20; Associated Press (cover);
Camera Press 7 (Novosti), 8, 39 (Donald
McCullin/ILN); Howard Davies, Exile Images
(contents) (top), 21, 24, 30, 31, 32, 44, 45; The
Illustrated London News Picture Library 34; The
John F. Kennedy Library 40; Peter Newark's
Military Pictures 10; Popperfoto (imprint page),
(contents) (bottom) (Jason Reed, Reuters), 4, 5
(Nayef Hashlamoun, Reuters), 6, 11 (Corinne
Dufka, Reuters), 12 (Jason Reed, Reuters), 15, 19,
22, 26, 27, 29 (Sukree Sukplang, Reuters), 33 (Greg
Bos, Reuters), 35 (Faleh Kheibar, Reuters), 37
(Jayanta Shaw, Reuters), 38 (Laszlo Balogh,
Reuters), 41 (White House, Reuters), 42, 43 (Ulli
Michel, Reuters); Topham Picturepoint 9 (P. de
Jong, Associated Press), 13, 14, 16, 17 (J. Gapps,
Associated Press), 18 (Associated Press), 23 (J.
Delay, STR), 25 (Press Association), 28, 36 (D.
Brauchli, Associated Press).

Cover picture: A US Blackhawk helicopter taking
part in a military exercise in Bosnia in 1996.

Contents

1. Wars and warring   4

2. Fighting wars   10

3. Types of wars   16

4. Rules of war   22

5. The impact of war   28

6. Questions about wars   34

7. Intervention and mediation   40

Glossary   46
Further information   47
Index   48

1. Wars and warring

What is war?

One way to define war is to say that it is legalized violence. Traditionally it occurs when the people of one country fight against the people of another country; or, in the case of civil war, when groups within a country fight each other. Actions that would be criminal offences in peacetime are considered acceptable – even courageous – during a war.

It is not easy to say when a skirmish or fighting becomes a war. War is not something that has a clear definition but it is usually 'declared' by a political leader who has power and authority, and is a state of affairs that is recognized by both sides and by other countries.

▼ *Women are members of armies of most countries. These soldiers are taking part in a military parade in Tiananmen Square in Beijing, China.*

In modern wars it has become increasingly difficult to recognize who the opposing forces are because many conflicts now take place within countries and often involve criminal gangs. The fighting may be intense but if war is not officially declared, soldiers and civilians cannot benefit from the protection of the various international conventions that exist. Their actions are then seen as acts of terrorism and are considered illegal. In these circumstances it is also more difficult to end a war as either side may refuse to accept peace treaties and carry on fighting.

Even though war legalizes various acts of violence, and despite the saying 'All's fair in love and war', acts against civilians and violent acts of unnecessary brutality, such as torture, are ruled to be crimes by international courts.

▲ Young people and children are often involved in fighting. On the West Bank a young Palestinian armed with stones approaches Israeli troops.

FACT:
Worldwide there are about 23 million soldiers. Israel has most per head of population with 41 for every 1,000 citizens; the USA, France, Britain and Australia each have around 12 per 1,000 citizens.
Worldwatch Institute, State of the World 1998

5

A brief history of war

People have been fighting wars for as long as history has been recorded. The earliest known wars were fought for food and land on a very small scale between hunters and farmers using clubs, spears and stones. As civilization has developed, so too has war and the reasons why people fight have become more complex.

In the nineteenth century, for the first time, wars were fought by industrial nations. They used the power of science and technology to make rifles, machine guns and artillery on a huge scale. Using these weapons and fleets of warships, European countries were able to dominate land and trade around the world and establish their empires. Empires brought great wealth to countries such as Britain and Germany.

By 1914 these imperial powers had formed two huge alliances that fought each other in the First World War. Soldiers fought hand-to-hand in the trenches. By the outbreak of the Second World War in 1939, bombing from the air and long-range artillery kept armies further apart and distant from the destruction and death their weapons caused, resulting in a huge increase in the number of civilian casualties.

▼ *During the First World War women worked in munitions factories, proving that they could do the hard physical work that men had previously done.*

During the second half of the twentieth century the threat of weapons of mass destruction, particularly the nuclear bomb, led to a stand-off between the main superpowers – the United States and the Soviet Union. Each embarked on an 'arms race', investing more and more money in the development of destructive weapons, but without ever actually going to war. This period was known as the 'Cold War'. It came to an end in the 1990s when political tension between the superpowers lessened after the break-up of the Soviet Union and treaties were signed agreeing to reduce the stockpile of weapons in the world.

▲ The May Day parade in Red Square, Moscow was when the Soviet Union displayed its military might.

FACT:
In 1986 the global stockpile of nuclear warheads peaked at 69,490 – the equivalent of 3.6 tonnes of TNT for every human being in the world.
New Internationalist, *December 2000*

Why do wars start?

No single answer is adequate to explain what causes wars to happen in a particular place at a particular time. But wars do not just occur – they are started by people.

Although wars inevitably lead to suffering and death, some people benefit from wars. A war can provide a reason for a country to unite behind a leader and increase her or his popularity. After the Falklands War in 1982, the popularity of Margaret Thatcher, the Prime Minister of Britain, increased dramatically. Political leaders who feel that they are losing their people's support sometimes start wars as an excuse for not holding an election that may result in their downfall.

Countries fight wars to improve their standing in the world, their trading opportunities and to increase their territory. People fight wars to defend themselves, because they are fearful and because they are desperately looking for ways to improve their lives. However, the results of war are usually so devastating that few benefit.

▼ *The British Prime Minister, Margaret Thatcher, welcomes back to the UK the Task Force ships that had been fighting in the Falklands War.*

Different ideologies and beliefs have been a cause of wars for hundreds of years. The second half of the twentieth century saw the ideologies of communism and capitalism pitted against one another, leading to the Korean and Vietnam Wars. Religious differences have been a factor in many conflicts, including the Arab-Israeli Wars.

It is difficult to understand fully why people fight wars. The reasons are many, complex and often rooted in history. Looking at some examples of wars and listening to people who have been involved in them may help our understanding.

▲ *Women, children and other civilians have increasingly become involved in the effects of wars. This is a street in Grozny, the capital of Chechnya, in 1996.*

2. Fighting wars

Why do people fight?

When war breaks out most young men have little choice about whether they will fight or not. Conscription comes into force which means that they are compelled to join the military – in Israel this requirement includes young women as well. People may be excused service in some countries if they are unfit or ill, or believe for religious or humanitarian reasons that it is wrong to fight. Otherwise they can be jailed, or, in some countries, even executed, if they refuse to go to war.

During the Vietnam War in the 1960s and 1970s many young American men refused to join the army because they disagreed with the reasons why that war was being fought. They publicly burned their draft papers. Some were sent to prison while others fled over the border into Canada to escape the authorities until the war was over.

When people are desperately poor, it is easy for them to blame others for their suffering and to take any measures that may improve their lives. They may believe that fighting will help them achieve a more prosperous life, although this is rarely the case. War is more likely to happen when there are no peaceful ways to escape from poverty.

▼ *This poster, protesting against the Vietnam War, is based on a First World War recruiting poster which read 'I Want You for the US Army'.*

Some people actually enjoy the excitement and adventure of fighting – and possibly even killing. Some of these people find it very difficult to adjust to civilian life once a war is over and so they become mercenaries – people who offer their services as soldiers to whoever will pay them.

▲ *These troops from the Comoros Islands, which are near Madagascar in the Indian Ocean, are led by a mercenary soldier from France in 1995.*

case study · case study · case study · case study · case study

Pedro, a young man in El Salvador, was on his way home from visiting some friends one evening when he was stopped at an army checkpoint. He was ordered off the bus and taken to the barracks. He was forcibly recruited into the army although he was only 16. He was trained for four months and was then sent out to fight. He was told that if he did not fight, the guerrilla rebels would kill him. He spent three months in hospital after he was injured but he never understood who or why he was fighting.

Why do children fight?

It is estimated that there are 300,000 child soldiers around the world in countries as far apart as Sierra Leone, Burma and Afghanistan. Some child soldiers are as young as six years old and many of them are girls.

Modern infantry weapons are simple to operate and very light, so children can easily use them. Armies like to recruit children because they are cheap to feed, easy to influence and often fearless in the face of the enemy. This is probably because they do not realize what is happening. Some children have said that they only killed small children as they believed this was a less serious wrongdoing than killing adults.

▼ *This 12-year-old boy is part of a rebel army fighting against the military government in Burma in 2000.*

Young schoolchildren parading in military uniforms in Angola. Children as young as this cannot understand what war is about.

In the civil war in Sierra Leone between 1991 and 1999, up to 20,000 children fought on both sides. Many were abducted from their villages after they had witnessed, or even been forced to take part in, the killing of their families. They were drugged and forced to fight. Some children become soldiers in order to get food and security, or to avenge the deaths of their families.

It is hard to assess the kind of long-term damage these children will suffer and how they can be rehabilitated into a peaceful society. Special care centres have been set up in Sierra Leone to help rehabilitate children who have been involved in war. They are counselled and given the help and support they need to return to a normal life.

The recruitment of children under 15 is now recognized as a war crime and those responsible for recruiting them can be tried at the International Court of Justice in The Hague.

> 'When I was killing, I felt like it wasn't me doing these things. I had to because the rebels threatened to kill me'
>
> *Peter, aged 12, who had been abducted by rebel forces during Sierra Leone's internal armed conflict.*

War and new technology

Computers and information technology have created new systems that can guide missiles, bombs and artillery shells with almost absolute precision. Guided by satellites, computer maps and laser beams, these munitions can be steered to strike almost any target - a tank, military headquarters or an airfield. Although these systems are not perfect and can fail, just like a home computer, when they do work they are capable of hitting a target the size of a door from hundreds, or even thousands, of miles away.

Armed forces increasingly rely on computer technology to direct these kinds of weapons and also to access and transmit information about the enemy. A modern soldier is as likely to be a computer expert as a tank driver. If the computer systems fail, or are affected by computer viruses, the consequences can be disastrous.

> FACT:
> The United States of America is the world's biggest arms exporter supplying around 40 per cent of the developing world's arms and ammunition.

◄ *A US commander stands watch over computers at the North American Aerospace Defense Command. This is housed in a vast chamber inside Cheyenne Mountain in Colorado to protect the computers from the effects of nuclear attack.*

Hackers are now giving military authorities cause for concern. Hackers are people who try to take control of other computers by using the telephone lines that computers use to communicate with other computers. Hackers have broken into US and UK government computers as well as those of big companies such as Microsoft.

Many people believe that future wars will involve battles in cyberspace with countries, terrorist groups and even individuals fighting across the Internet. During the 1999 Kosovo crisis it is believed that the US experts hacked into the Serbian air defence system computers, making it safer for US bombers to attack their targets.

▲ *Three batteries of the US-made Patriot missiles in Saudi Arabia during the Gulf War in 1991. The weapons are designed to shoot down incoming enemy missiles in mid-air.*

3. Types of wars

Land and resources

Land is vital to people. They need it to grow food and as a source of water. Rivers flow, regardless of national boundaries, from one country to another and conflicts can be caused if the water supply is interfered with – for example, if the water is taken or polluted before it reaches neighbouring countries.

Often land has some historical importance. It may be where people's ancestors lived or it may have a religious significance. This is the case in the Middle East where Jews and Arabs have fought for years over territory that both sides claim is their natural homeland.

▼ British troops during the war with Argentina over the sovereignty of the Falkland Islands in the South Atlantic in 1982. Over 1,000 soldiers died during this conflict.

Land is also the source of precious resources such as building materials, deposits of energy like oil and gas, and precious metals such as gold and diamonds. Trade wars have been fought over all these resources. In the past, wars were also fought over commodities, such as salt and spices, that nowadays are commonplace, but that at the time were rare and highly prized.

Modern wars are more likely to be fought over oil, water and new technology, or to prevent the international trade of drugs such as heroin.

Oil has become such an essential part of modern life that several conflicts have arisen because of it. In 1991 Iraq claimed that Kuwait was a province of Iraq and invaded. An alliance of Western countries, led by the United States and acting with the approval of the United Nations, launched Operation Desert Storm and expelled Iraqi forces from Kuwait after a short war. It was the strategic importance of Kuwait as one of the world's main oil-producing countries that led the alliance to spring so quickly to Kuwait's defence.

▼ The deliberate burning of oil wells as the Iraqi troops retreated at the end of the Gulf War in 1991 created enormous environmental problems.

Colonialism

As long as nations have been fighting to gain control over other countries, people have fought back for the right to enjoy self-determination and to govern themselves.

In the first half of the twentieth century many countries in Africa and Asia were still colonies of European powers. Between the 1940s and the 1960s several of them gained their independence. Some, such as Kenya and India, became independent after rebellions and revolts, but without outright war. But the desire to be independent led to several long and brutal conflicts. Algeria's struggle for independence from France lasted from 1954 until 1962, while the people of Mozambique fought for over ten years before they gained their independence from Portugal in 1974.

▲ *French troops move onto the streets of Algiers in 1962 in response to local demands for independence for Algeria.*

But, in addition to wars of independence, colonialism led to other kinds of wars too. At the end of the nineteenth century the European powers had arbitrarily drawn the borders of African countries with little regard to the wide variety of different ethnic groups that lived there, thereby sowing the seeds of future conflicts.

Some ethnic groups found that they lived on either side of the new borders, while others found themselves in the same country as old enemies. Once these countries became independent, tensions sometimes erupted between the different groups. In the newly independent Nigeria, for example, the Igbo people in the south-east of the country attempted to become a separate state and fighting broke out in July 1967. The breakaway state, called Biafra, had insufficient resources to fight a war and more than one million people are thought to have died as a result of the conflict.

'Living in Biafra was like living in hell. We lived in bombed-out buildings, abandoned school classrooms or refugee camps. We stood in long lines to receive relief foods flown into Biafra by charity organizations.'
Grace Asika, a Biafran refugee

▶ *A heavily armed soldier in 1967, during the Biafran War in Nigeria.*

Exploiting fear

When people feel threatened, or are in difficult circumstances, they may look for someone to blame for their problems or feel that they can act recklessly because they have nothing left to lose. In these circumstances ruthless leaders can exploit people and encourage them to pick on anyone who is different from them. It may be because their religion is different, because they look different or have a different lifestyle.

In Germany during the 1930s the economy began to fail and people found they were becoming poorer. They became anxious about the future. Hitler's Nazi government issued a lot of propaganda saying that the Jews were to blame. This helped Nazi fascist policies to be accepted by the German people, which paved the way for the Holocaust of the Second World War and the deaths of six million Jews.

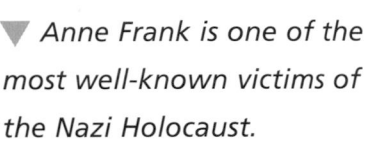

▼ Anne Frank is one of the most well-known victims of the Nazi Holocaust.

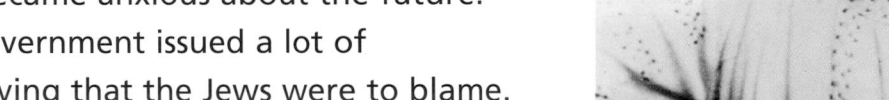

case study · case study · case study · case study · case study

Anne Frank and her family, who were Jewish, fled to the Netherlands during the Second World War and hid for nearly two years from the Nazis in a neighbour's attic in Amsterdam. Anne kept a diary of her thoughts and fears about being persecuted and also about her everyday life. The family was eventually discovered, captured and taken to concentration camps. In 1945 Anne died in Belsen concentration camp, aged 14. Her diary, which was published after the war, showed her great courage.

Between 1975 and 1979, the regime of Pol Pot in Cambodia claimed the lives of more than one million people. His army, the Khmer Rouge, tried to wipe out any signs of the modern world. He declared 1975 was 'year zero'. Anyone who was considered an intellectual or educated, even if they only wore glasses or were able to speak another language, might be killed. These massacres came to be known as the time of 'The Killing Fields'.

These wars are often the most shocking and distressful because friends and neighbours end up fighting one another, often with little understanding of why they are doing so. It takes many decades for countries to come to terms with what has happened.

FACT: Cambodia has the world's highest rate of orphans and widows as a result of the actions of Pol Pot's horrific regime in the 1970s.

These human skulls are part of the Choeung Ek memorial to the people killed by the Khmer Rouge.

4. Rules of war

War crimes

War crimes are those actions taken during a time of war that target civilians or use unnecessary violence, cruelty and torture against soldiers and prisoners of war. Some of the most horrendous crimes ever committed by human beings have taken place during wartime. Why do people, some of whom in civilian life would not think of committing such acts, do such terrible things? It is well known that the violence of war can desensitize people so that they do not understand what they are doing. They shut off a part of their brains from realizing what is happening. Others may take advantage of the confusion of war, believing their crimes will go unnoticed. And, indeed, it is notoriously difficult to bring people to court for war crimes.

War in the twentieth century was characterized by terrible crimes against humanity, such as mass murder, genocide and ethnic cleansing.

In November 1969, during the Vietnam War, 567 unarmed Vietnamese peasants, mainly women and children, were massacred in the village of My Lai by American soldiers.

▼ *William Calley, who was found guilty by court martial for his part in the My Lai massacre, leaving court in April 1971.*

In their defence all the soldiers claimed that they were only obeying orders given by their superiors. Although one of the officers spent four years in prison for what happened, all charges were dropped against the others involved.

Pictures of emaciated prisoners held in Serbian prison camps shocked the world in 1992. The Serbs conducted a policy of ethnic cleansing which entailed removing all non-Serbs from the areas they dominated. This policy reminded many people of the actions of the Nazis against the Jews during the Holocaust in the 1940s.

FACT:
In 1999 the spending on the armed forces of Europe and North America alone was $US520 billion - more than double the entire annual income of all the people of Russia.
Stockholm International Peace Research Institute

Ratko Mladic, a former Bosnian Serb general, has been charged with genocide for killing up to 6,000 Muslims in Srebrenica in July 1995.

War and international law

Rules governing warfare have existed for thousands of years. The Ancient Egyptians, Greeks and Romans had clear codes of conduct, although they did not always follow them. The Bible, the Qur'an and other sacred texts of the major religions also contain laws advocating respect for enemies. But as long as rules have existed, they have also been broken.

▼ *An International Red Cross member takes care of an unaccompanied Rwandan refugee child in Zaire in 1997.*

In 1859 a young Swiss banker, Henri Dunant, witnessed the terrible suffering of wounded soldiers during the Battle of Solferino. He campaigned for better treatment of the wounded in warfare. Eventually this led to the creation of the Geneva Conventions, which laid down rules about standards of care and the treatment of prisoners, civilians and prisoners of war. The International Red Cross was set up to be the official guardian of the Geneva Conventions, and, alongside the Islamic Red Crescent, it has grown into an international movement.

Since the Second World War, international law has been increasingly concerned with the protection of human rights, particularly in line with the United Nations Universal Declaration of Human Rights of 1948 and a convention designed to prevent and punish those committing genocide.

The International Court of Justice or World Court was created in 1945 to try and resolve disputes between countries before conflict developed. However, the power of the Court depends on countries complying with its rulings. In the past the United States, the Soviet Union, China, France, Italy and Germany have refused to accept its authority.

▲ *The Geneva Conventions state that prisoners of war should be well treated. These Second World War prisoners at Colditz Castle in Germany are enjoying a game of volleyball.*

Enforcing the rules

As crimes such as genocide, mass murder and rape used as weapons of war have become more widespread, the 'international community' has recognized the need to punish those responsible.

The International Military Tribunal at Nuremberg was set up in 1945, in the wake of the Second World War, to bring to trial those Nazis responsible for the organized and systematic killing of Jews, gypsies and homosexuals. This was the first time that individuals had been held to account for their wartime actions. Several Nazis were found guilty and sentenced to death.

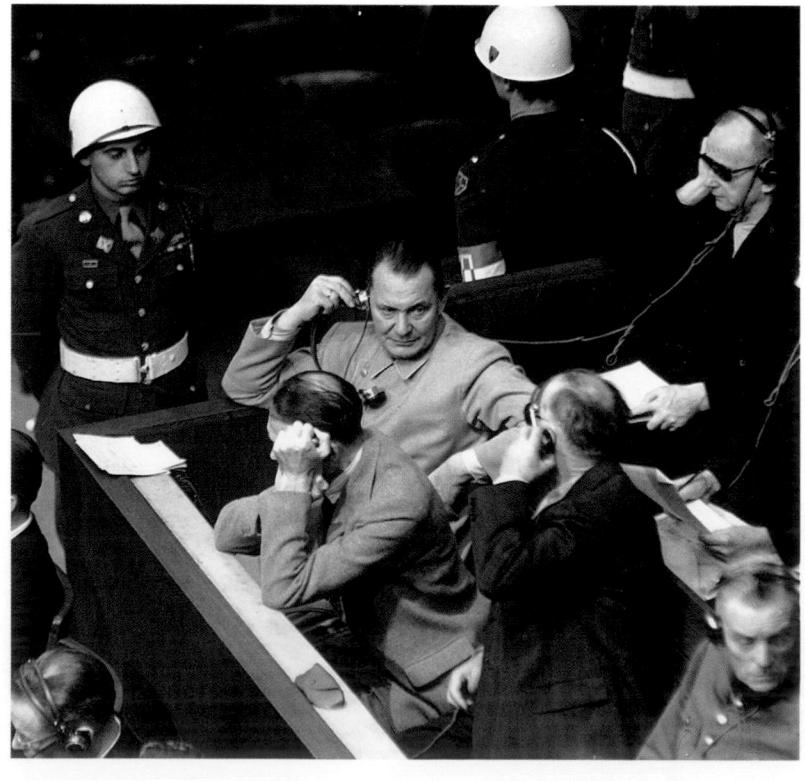

◄ *Hermann Goering (facing camera) talks to fellow accused Nazis at the Nuremberg war crimes trial in October 1946.*

Hermann Goering, one of Hitler's right-hand men, committed suicide in prison just a few hours before he was due to be executed for his war crimes. More than 50 years after the end of the Second World War, alleged war criminals are still being brought to trial. In 1991, the UK War Crimes Act ruled that people living in Britain who had committed war crimes could be tried there for their crimes even though they had taken place in a different country.

> 'I feel that justice should be done so that other people should not have similar experiences. Those who did these things should be punished for what they have done. We see people walking around who did things to us and we don't even know if anything is going to be done to them.'
>
> *Uwambeyi Esperance, whose husband and baby were killed in 1994 in Rwanda*

After many conflicts, when it is suspected that atrocities have taken place, the United Nations holds an International Criminal Tribunal to name and try those who have allegedly committed war crimes. At the tribunal following the massacres in Rwanda, some of the defendants were children. Slobodan Milosevic, the Serbian leader at the time of the policy of ethnic cleansing in the former Yugoslavia, was indicted for war crimes and was arrested in Belgrade in April 2001.

◀ *In 1998 General Pinochet was held in Britain for alleged crimes that he had committed in Chile following the military coup he led in 1973. He was eventually allowed to return safely to Chile for health reasons.*

27

5. The impact of war

Civilians and war

The technology of modern warfare has reduced the need for soldiers to fight face-to-face and hand-to-hand. Unfortunately though, as weapons have become capable of striking at longer ranges, civilians have become more vulnerable to attack.

During the First World War, only five per cent of casualties were civilians. In wars at the end of the twentieth century this number had risen to over eighty per cent, most of whom were women and children. Currently, more children than armed soldiers are killed or disabled by war.

International law states that soldiers should be able to discriminate between using weapons against other soldiers – the enemy – and civilians. But landmines cannot tell the difference between the footfall of a soldier or a child herding animals or playing. Landmines can lie hidden in the ground for years after a battle has been fought, and people have returned to their homes and land. As a result, thousands of innocent people have been killed or maimed by stepping on landmines.

▼ *Phan Thi Kim Phuc was nine years old when she was photographed screaming in pain from burns caused by napalm during the Vietnam War. Today she is a goodwill ambassador for the United Nations. She said, 'Let the world see how horrible war can be.'*

Many members of the Cambodian paralympic basketball team (in blue vests) are the victims of landmines that were laid in their country during several years of war.

Increasingly, civilians are being regarded as legitimate targets in warfare. Humanitarian convoys, hospitals, health clinics, and feeding stations have all been the targets of attacks. In Chechnya in 1999, Red Cross workers found that even children had been deliberately shot through the head.

Chemical and biological weapons kill by spreading poisons or disease over a wide area, killing or infecting everyone in their path. Although most countries in the world have agreed never to use them, they nevertheless were used by Japan against China in 1942, and by Iraq against Kurdish rebels in the 1980s. On both occasions the victims were civilians who died in large numbers.

FACT:
In the last decade more than two million children have died as a result of war and up to five million have been disabled. Each month 2,000 men, women and children are killed, blinded or lose a limb because of landmines.
Department for International Development

Refugees

Refugees are found in every country of the world but most live in the poorer countries of the developing world. Refugees are civilians who are forced to leave their homes because of war and conflict. Often they have to leave at very short notice and are only able to take a few possessions with them. Many of them are never able to return, or return only many years later to find their homes destroyed. Refugees often find it hard to find a country willing to take them in and they can spend months or years being bounced back and forth between nations.

The largest group of refugees are the five million Afghans who left their homeland following the Soviet occupation between 1979 and 1989 and settled in Pakistan and Iran.

Following the war in 1948 that established the state of Israel, 200,000 Palestinians fled to neighbouring Arab countries and to the Gaza Strip and West Bank, areas that were occupied by Israel in 1967.

▼ *Children growing up in refugee camps in Gaza have spent their lives in close contact with conflict and violence. How can this pattern be broken?*

The United Nations High Commission for Refugees (UNHCR) was created in 1951 to resettle refugees still remaining in European displaced persons' camps after the Second World War. Its job has grown dramatically as the number of refugees has increased as a result of some 250 conflicts around the world. In 1954 and again in 1981 UNHCR won the Nobel Peace Prize for its work in protecting the rights of refugees.

FACT:
Of the approximately 17 million refugees in the world:
7.6 million are in Iran and Pakistan, North Africa and the Middle East
5.4 million are in Africa south of the Sahara
2.4 million are in Europe and the USA
1.2 million are in Latin America and the Caribbean
0.6 million are in the rest of Asia

UNHCR, 1999

◄ *The UNHCR returns Tamil refugees to their homes in Sri Lanka in 1995.*

case study · case study · case study · case study · case study

Wali is ten years old. He was born in Afghanistan and for the first few years of his life he went to school, played football and was happy like any other young boy. But one night men came to his house and took his father away and shot him. Fighting broke out in the city all around his family. Reluctantly they realized they would have to leave their home if they were to survive. Wali and his family now live in London.

After the war

The physical injuries that result from wars are often plain to see, especially in countries like Angola and Cambodia where it is common to see young men in wheelchairs and children on crutches, victims of war and landmines. But war can also have a devastating effect beyond the physical suffering.

Soldiers sometimes return from wars showing symptoms of mental disturbance and they may be almost unrecognizable as the person they used to be. They might have a short temper, have difficulty knowing where they are and suffer from depression. This used to be known as 'shell-shock' but was later called post-traumatic stress disorder. Its effects can be so severe that sufferers can no longer work.

▲ Soldiers like these, injured by landmines in Sri Lanka, will have to learn new ways of leading their lives and earning a living.

case study · case study · case study · case study · case study

Berta Ngheve, a 23-year-old Angolan, was walking with her sister near her home to find food when she stepped on a mine. She had no idea the path was dangerous. She heard a huge noise and then there was a terrible silence. A few seconds later she looked at her leg and realized that it was no longer there. Her daily chores – collecting water and firewood and preparing food – are more difficult to do. Berta now works as a tailor.

Poor countries that are ravaged by war often suffer famine. The war means that food cannot be distributed and the land cannot be farmed properly. The Ethiopian famine of 1984 was caused by a combination of a drought and war.

The environment also suffers in other ways too. During the Vietnam War, the US troops used Agent Orange – a chemical that affects plants and causes them to lose their leaves. This made it more difficult for the Vietnamese fighters to hide in the jungles and deprived the civilian population of food crops. It also contaminated fish and water supplies. The land was left contaminated and 25 years after the end of the Vietnam War, the Vietnamese people still have difficulty growing the food crops they need to live.

▼ *Remembering wars, and fellow soldiers killed, is very important to many ex-soldiers. Remembering may also help others understand the lessons wars teach us.*

6. Questions about wars

Can war ever be justified?

Huge arguments exist about whether going to war can ever be justified.

On the one hand, pacifists argue that violence can never be justified in any circumstances. Believers in this philosophy included the Indian leader Mahatma Gandhi, who opposed all kinds of violence. His life was dedicated to gaining independence for India but instead of advocating fighting, he undertook a programme of 'satyagraha' or non-violent resistance. His ideas quickly spread through India – people resigned from their jobs, the courts were boycotted and children were withdrawn from school. Gandhi believed that the British would eventually consider violence useless and leave India – which they did in 1947.

▲ *Mahatma Gandhi is still respected today for his stance against violence.*

Often sanctions are used to take action against countries as an alternative to fighting. Sanctions against Iraq have been in place since the war in 1991 but these have led to a huge decline in health care because of shortages in the supply of medicines and vaccinations. The incidence of diseases in children has also increased. This is a different form of warfare that strikes hardest at the young and vulnerable.

◀ *Ten years of UN sanctions against Iraq have forced many Iraqis to sell their belongings to raise cash to pay for their families' medical needs. This is an open-air market in Baghdad in 2001.*

On the other hand, there are those who argue that force is justified if it reduces suffering and injustice, or if it is used in self-defence, or to protect the weak. This latter argument was put forward by the religious scholar St Thomas Aquinas in the thirteenth century and his ideas still influence the way in which most Western political and military leaders seek to justify military actions. People who believe that wars can be justified would offer the fight against the injustice of apartheid in South Africa as a good example of a justifiable war.

66

'Fight in the cause of Allah against those who fight you, but do not transgress limits.'
From the Qur'an, the holy book of Islam
(in other words it is permitted to fight in self-defence)

99

More than fighting?

Many of the men and women who join the military forces never actually have to go to war and fight, although they see a lot of action.

After the Second World War it was widely believed that a war like that should never happen again. The United Nations (UN) was formed in 1945 to promote world peace and prosperity. One of its main aims was to prevent future wars by intervention at an early stage through a mixture of diplomacy and the use of soldiers to keep the peace. The UN soldiers, drawn from the armies of all members, wear distinctive light blue berets or helmets and usually carry only light weapons. Their task is to separate the warring sides and enforce peace. But it requires all members of the UN Security Council to agree that they should intervene in a dispute, which is not always possible. This has left countries like Chechnya, in conflict with Russia, without the protection of UN peacekeepers.

Soldiers nowadays often play a major role in relief work when natural or man-made disasters strike. The skills and equipment involved in planning and fighting wars can be turned to help the victims of floods, earthquakes and hurricanes. Aircraft from many different air forces help to drop food and medical supplies.

▼ *A British United Nations soldier watches for sniper fire while helping to carry the bags of a Bosnian Croat refugee as she is evacuated in 1993. As a UN soldier, he may only use his gun in self-defence.*

▲ *Indian soldiers help to search the collapsed buildings for bodies and to clear the rubble following the massive earthquake in Bhuj in February 2001.*

A new development is the USA's plan to send advisers, weapons and funds to support the Colombian army in its fight against drug producers. The US government plans to spend more than 1 billion dollars on training, helicopters, surveillance planes and bases in drug-producing areas.

FACT:
The United States currently accounts for four per cent of United Nations forces and ranks sixteenth behind Bangladesh, Ghana, Nepal and Fiji in troop contributions.
United Nations, 1999

Are wars reported accurately?

Our televisions and newspapers are full of pictures and stories of war from many parts of the world. It is the job of journalists, TV crews and photographers to inform the public about what is going on. Photography started to play an important role in the reporting of war as long ago as the American Civil War (1861-65) and the Crimean War (1853-55).

Journalists have traditionally acted as eye-witnesses and independent observers, often risking their own lives to find information and take pictures. They believe that objectivity is the key to the reporter's ability to inform the public and act as a watchdog.

▼ *A Bosnian Serb officer tries to prevent a TV crew from filming at a United Nations-held airport in Sarajevo in 1995. Armies are very sensitive about releasing information that may help the other side.*

But as Winston Churchill said 'The first casualty of war is truth'. Governments are not always happy for the public to know what really happens in wartime. During the Vietnam War in the 1960s, television coverage had the opposite effect from the one the US government wanted. People saw explicit pictures of the horrors of modern warfare for the first time and public opinion swung to become extremely critical of America's involvement in the war.

Propaganda is a powerful weapon in a war and each side is very concerned to make sure that the public are hearing what the authorities want them to hear. During the Second World War, Lord Haw Haw, an Anglo-Irishman who supported Nazi Germany, made radio broadcasts from Germany to listeners in Britain trying to frighten them and cause general panic. He was eventually hanged for treason in 1946. Governments have used cartoons, postcards, cinema advertising and even dropped leaflets from aeroplanes to get their message across.

▲ *This photograph was taken by the famous war photographer Don McCullin during the Vietnam War. His photos showed what war was like for ordinary soldiers and civilians caught up in fighting and violence.*

> ❝
> 'I do not believe we should stand neutrally between good and evil, right and wrong, aggressor and victim.'
> *Martin Bell, BBC reporter, calling on the BBC to abandon neutrality in reporting war*
> ❞

7. Intervention and mediation

Preventing war and negotiating peace

With a world population of over six billion, there are more people sharing the planet than ever before. Weapons are more numerous and effective and the threat of war is always present. Despite all this, governments around the world seem more prepared to put effort and resources into making and keeping peace. This may be because they realize what the awful consequences would be if they do not.

In November 1962 many people feared that the USA and Soviet Union would go to war over Soviet nuclear missiles based in Cuba, an island friendly to the Soviets that was only 160 kilometres from the US mainland.

> FACT:
> The START-II Treaty signed by USA and Russia in January 1993 set a ceiling of 3,500 nuclear warheads for both of these countries, this limit to be achieved by 2003 at the latest.
> *US Bureau of Public Affairs, 1996*

▶ *The US and Soviet leaders, John Kennedy and Nikita Khrushchev, at a meeting in Vienna, Austria in the early 1960s. The two leaders managed to avoid going to war when the Cuban Missile Crisis threatened world peace.*

The US president, John Kennedy, and Soviet premier, Nikita Khrushchev, negotiated over Kennedy's demand that the missiles must be removed and that ships carrying more weapons to Cuba should turn back. Both men were told by their military advisers to be prepared for nuclear war but they came to an agreement in which they both made concessions. Official records from the time show that the world was only minutes away from war.

Negotiation has also worked in smaller conflicts that are still very serious. In South Africa, Israel and Palestine, and Northern Ireland, a fragile peace has been maintained by keeping talks going and exploring all avenues for agreement. Often a third country will chair the talks and act as a go-between for the opposing sides. This is called mediation.

▼ *US President Clinton acting as a go-between for Israeli Prime Minister Barak and Palestinian President Yasser Arafat in July 2000.*

Rebuilding homes, rebuilding trust

The effects of war do not end when the fighting does. Any war, large or small, damages people and places. Much rebuilding needs to take place so that people can carry on with their lives and not fear that another war may suddenly break out again.

At the end of the Second World War much of Europe, especially Germany, stood in ruins. Although people were relieved to see the end of the fighting, they knew that a huge rebuilding job lay ahead. Some people wanted to see Germany totally destroyed as a punishment for having started the war. The Allies realized, though, that Germany would have to be rebuilt to avoid creating conditions of misery and poverty that might push its desperate people into starting another war. The USA funded much of the reconstruction, spending billions of dollars in creating a new Europe. This programme of aid was known as 'The Marshall Plan' after the US Secretary of State, George Marshall.

▼ *After the Second World War, much rebuilding work took place in Germany to help revitalize the economy. This picture shows a new hotel being built in Berlin.*

case study · case study · case study · case study · case study

At the village of Neve Shalom~Wahat al Salam in northern Israel, young Arab and Israelis study side by side. This is in a country where conflict between the two peoples has been going on for over fifty years and it is rare for Arabs and Israelis to mix. The village runs its own school and organizes courses for young Arab and Israeli students where they come together to talk and share their lives with one another for a few days. Shani, a 17-year-old Jewish girl said 'We met, we listened and we learned that Jews and Arabs are the same.'

In 1994, following South Africa's first democratic election, Nelson Mandela was elected as the President of South Africa. The previous leaders of South Africa had imprisoned him for 25 years for his opposition to apartheid. Many other South Africans had been imprisoned or killed by the apartheid regime, but Mandela did not seek revenge. He felt that reconciliation could be brought about by openness, honesty and forgiveness. His government established The Truth and Reconciliation Commission and promised an amnesty to all those prepared to testify and admit their part in maintaining the system of apartheid.

◀ *Nelson Mandela salutes well-wishers as he leaves prison in 1990 after 25 years spent in captivity.*

Resolving conflicts

Conflict is a factor that is present in everyone's daily life, from disagreements over which television programme to watch to arguing which is the best sports team. Conflicts in everyday life can be sorted out by negotiation and compromise, just as disagreements between countries can be sorted out in the same way. In both cases, if this approach fails, the consequences rarely benefit either of the warring parties.

Just as governments may ask the United Nations, or another country, to bring two sides together to discuss their differences, so young people may ask a friend, a teacher or a parent for guidance or a ruling in a dispute. Adults may refer a disagreement to an arbitrator or a small court to settle the matter. This is always preferable to letting hostility and violence rule the outcome.

▼ *A United Nations soldier from Ethiopia helps move refugees on the Rwanda-Zaire border in Africa in 1994.*

It is important for all societies that solutions are sought to resolve conflict peacefully through the courts and, where they exist, democratic institutions such as Parliament, Congress and state legislatures.

▲ In this puppet show, put on by the United Nations Children's Fund (UNICEF) in Burundi, the puppets are being used to show children how they can work through and reconcile their differences.

Many young people in schools across the world are learning about conflict resolution. Citizenship and civics lessons are providing knowledge through examples, such as those examined in this book. In many schools young people are learning about conflict resolution through the experience of being involved in mediation schemes where they help to resolve conflicts between other students.

case study · case study · case study · case study · case study

Claire Gerrens is a 15-year-old pupil at Tanfield School in Durham, UK. She volunteered for the school's mediation scheme, which was suggested by a student who saw a similar scheme on a visit to Colorado, USA. After a training course Claire joined the team of young people who mediate between fellow pupils unable to resolve conflicts. They sit with the two people and encourage them to listen and talk to each other. 'It really works,' says Claire. 'I've seen people who couldn't talk without fighting really try hard to be friends. It helps to make all of us more confident about solving problems like this.'

GLOSSARY

Alliance
An agreement between countries to co-operate with each other in a friendly way.

Amnesty
A promise given by those in authority not to punish someone for a wrong or crime.

Apartheid
The system in South Africa that separated people because of their race and colour.

Arbitrator
Someone who listens to both sides of an argument and makes suggestions or recommendations to settle the argument.

Artillery
Heavy guns that fire large shells long distances.

Capitalism
An economic system based on the private ownership of wealth or capital.

Civilians
People who are not members of the military services.

Civil war
A war fought between two or more groups of people living in the same country.

Colonies
Territorial possessions owned by a ruling nation or state.

Communism
A political system that favours a classless society and the common ownership of property.

Conscription
Compulsory military service.

Draft papers
The official papers denoting compulsory military service in the USA.

Ethnic cleansing
The attempt to remove from a region, either through expulsion or murder, anyone who is of a different ethnic group.

Ethnic group
A group of people who share the same origins and lifestyle.

Genocide
The crime of destroying a national, ethnic, racial or religious group by mass murder.

Holocaust
An act of great destruction and loss of life. The term 'The Holocaust' refers to the attempt by Nazi Germany systematically to exterminate European Jews.

Humanitarian
Someone devoted to the promotion of human welfare.

Ideology
A system of political or philosophical beliefs.

International community
Co-operation between countries around the world to work together for peace.

Landmine
Explosive device buried in the ground designed to explode when a person steps on it.

Mercenaries
People hired to fight for a country other than their own.

Munitions
Weapons and military supplies.

Negotiations
Meetings where people or groups talk over their differences and try to reach an agreement that suits everyone.

Nobel Peace Prize
An award given every year to people or organizations who have advanced the cause of world peace.

Pacifist
Someone who is opposed to violence in any form and for any reason.

Propaganda
Information that is spread to further a particular cause.

Reconciliation
The process of bringing together, peacefully, former enemies or opponents.

Refugee
Someone who has to flee to another country, often because of conflict and persecution in their own land.

Rehabilitate
To help someone to return to a state of good health.

Sanctions
A way of forcing a country to do something by encouraging other countries not to trade with them.

Skirmish
A minor short-term fight.

Torture
The deliberate infliction of pain and suffering on a person.

Tribunal
A form of judicial court.

FURTHER INFORMATION

USEFUL ADDRESSES

In Australia
The Centre for Peace and
Conflict Studies
Mackie Building KO1
University of Sydney
Arundel Street
New South Wales 2006

In Europe
The International Federation
of Red Cross and Red
Crescent Societies
17 Chemin des Crets
Petit-Saconnex
PO Box 372
CH-1211 Geneva 19
Switzerland
www.ifrc.org

The Stockholm International
Peace Research Institute
Signalistgatan 9
SE – 169 70 Solna
Sweden
www.sipri.se

In the UK
Anne Frank Educational
Trust
PO Box 432
Bushey
Herts WD2 1QU

British Red Cross
10 Grosvenor Crescent
London SW1X 7EJ
www.redcross.org.uk

Centre for Conflict
Resolution
Department of Peace Studies
University of Bradford
West Yorkshire BD7 1DP
www.brad.ac.uk/acad/confres/

Quaker Peace and Service
Friends House
Euston Road
London NW1 2BJ

The Refugee Council
3 Bondway
London SW8 1SJ
www.refugeecouncil.org.uk

In the USA
Peace Action
1819 H St, NW
#420
Washington DC 2006

UNICEF
3 United Nations Plaza
New York 10017
www.unicef.org

US Committee for Refugees
1717 Massachusetts Ave NW
Suite 200
Washington DC 20036
www.refugees.org

learn.co.uk
from *The Guardian*
Visit learn.co.uk for more resources

BOOKS TO READ

*A Soldier's Life: A visual
history of soldiers through
the ages* by Andrew
Robertshaw, Heinemann
1997

*Famous Lives: Anne Frank:
Voice of Hope*, by Cath
Senker, Hodder Wayland
2000

One Day We Had To Run by
Sybella Wilkes: refugee
children tell their stories,
Evans Bros 1994

Points of View: Terrorism by
Alison Jamieson, Wayland
1991

The Breakup of Yugoslavia
by M. Rady, Wayland 1994

War: The World Reacts by
Paul Bennett, Belitha Press
1998

INDEX

Numbers in **bold** refer to pictures.

Afghans 30, 31
Algeria 18, **18**
Algiers **18**
American Civil War 38
Angola 32
apartheid 35
Arab-Israeli Wars 9, 30
Arafat, Yasser **41**

Barak, Prime Minister **41**
Biafra 19, **19**
biological weapons 29
Bosnia **36**, 41
Burundi **45**

Calley, William **22**
Cambodia 21, **21**, **29**, 32
Chechnya 29, 36
chemical weapons 29
child soldiers **5**, 12, **12**, 13, **13**
Churchill, Winston 39
civil war 4, 13
Clinton, President Bill **41**
'Cold War' 7
conscription 10
Crimean War 38

Dunant, Henri 24

Ethiopian famine 33
ethnic cleansing 22, 23

Falklands War 8, **8**, **16**
First World War 6, **6**, **10**, 28
Frank, Anne 20, **20**

Gandhi, Mahatma 34, **34**
Gaza **30**
Geneva Conventions 24, **25**

genocide 22, 25, 26
Goering, Hermann **26**, 27
Gulf War **15**, **17**

Haw Haw, Lord 39
Holocaust 20, **20**, 23
human rights 25

International Court of
    Justice 13, 25
International Military
    Tribunal 26
International Red Cross 24,
    24, 29
Iraq 29, **35**
Islamic Red Crescent 24

Jews 20, 23, 26

Kennedy, John 40, **40**, 41
Khmer Rouge 21, **21**
Khrushchev, Nikita 40, **40**, 41
Korean War 9
Kosovo crisis 15
Kurds 29
Kuwait 17, **17**

landmines 28, 29, **29**, 32, **32**

McCullin, Don **39**
Mandela, Nelson 43, **43**
'Marshall Plan' 42
mercenaries 11, **11**
Milosevic, Slobodan 27
Mladic, Ratko **23**
Mozambique 18
My Lai massacre 22, **22**

Nazis 20, 23, 26, **26**, 39
negotiation 40, 41, 44
Nobel Peace Prize 31
non-violent resistance 34

nuclear war 40

Phan Thi Kim Phuc **28**
Pinochet, General **27**
Pol Pot 21
prisoners of war 22, 24, **25**

Red Square, Moscow **7**
refugees **24**, 30, **30**, 31, **31**,
    36, **44**
rehabilitation 13
relief work by soldiers 36, **37**
Rwanda 27, **44**

sanctions 34, **35**
Second World War 6, 20, 25,
    25, 26, 27, 31, 36, 39, **42**
Serbs 23, **23**, **38**
Sierra Leone civil war 13
Sri Lanka **31**, **32**

television 38, **38**
terrorism 5
Thatcher, Margaret 8, **8**
torture 5, 22
trade wars 16

UN Commission for Refugees
    31, **31**
UN Security Council 36
UNICEF **45**
United Nations 27, **28**, 36,
    36, **38**, 44, **44**
Universal Declaration of
    Human Rights 25

Vietnam War 9, 10, **10**, 22,
    28, 33, 39, **39**

war crimes 13, 22, 23, **26**, 27
women and war **4**, **6**, **9**, 10
World Court 25